Beyond the Labels: Understanding the Spectrum of Bipolar Disorder

Mila Georgiev

Beyond the Labels: Understanding the Spectrum of Bipolar Disorder

Beyond the Labels: Understanding the Spectrum of Bipolar Disorder

Chapter 1: The Journey Begins

Understanding Bipolar Disorder: An Overview

Bipolar disorder is a complex mental health condition characterized by significant mood swings, including emotional highs known as mania or hypomania and lows referred to as depression. Understanding this disorder requires a compassionate approach, as it affects not only those diagnosed but also their families, friends, and caregivers. These mood changes can significantly impact daily life, relationships, and overall well-being. By exploring the nuances of bipolar disorder, we can foster a greater understanding and empathy for those navigating this challenging journey.

Beyond the Labels: Understanding the Spectrum of Bipolar Disorder

There are several distinct types of bipolar disorder, each presenting unique challenges and experiences. Bipolar I involves manic episodes that last at least seven days or are so severe that immediate hospital care is needed, while depressive episodes can occur as well. Bipolar II is characterized by a pattern of depressive episodes and hypomanic episodes, but without the full-blown manic episodes. Cyclothymic disorder involves periods of hypomanic symptoms and periods of depressive symptoms lasting for at least two years. Recognizing these variations can help patients and their loved ones tailor their approaches to treatment and support, ensuring that everyone involved understands the specific challenges that may arise.

Beyond the Labels: Understanding the Spectrum of Bipolar Disorder

Effective communication is essential in fostering healthy relationships with those affected by bipolar disorder. Family members and friends can learn strategies to express their support while also setting boundaries to protect their own emotional health. Open dialogues about feelings, triggers, and coping mechanisms can create a safe space for individuals to share their experiences. This understanding not only aids in crisis prevention but also strengthens the bond between loved ones, allowing for a more collaborative approach to managing the disorder.

Beyond the Labels: Understanding the Spectrum of Bipolar Disorder

Self-care for caregivers is equally important in this journey. The role of a caregiver can be both rewarding and challenging, often leading to feelings of stress and burnout. It is crucial for caregivers to prioritize their own mental and emotional well-being. Engaging in regular self-care practices, seeking support networks, and establishing personal boundaries are vital steps to ensure they can provide effective support without sacrificing their health. By nurturing themselves, caregivers can maintain the resilience needed to help their loved ones through the ups and downs of bipolar disorder.

Beyond the Labels: Understanding the Spectrum of Bipolar Disorder

Navigating the complexities of bipolar disorder is a shared journey that requires patience, understanding, and support. Building a robust support network involving family, friends, and professionals can significantly enhance the quality of life for those affected. By sharing personal stories and experiences, individuals can find solace in knowing they are not alone. Together, we can create an environment that promotes understanding, compassion, and resilience, empowering those with bipolar disorder and their loved ones to thrive despite the challenges they face.

The Importance of Compassionate Communication

Compassionate communication serves as the cornerstone for fostering understanding and connection among individuals affected by bipolar disorder. It transcends mere words, embodying a profound recognition of the emotions, struggles, and triumphs that both patients and their loved ones experience. When caregivers, family members, and friends engage in compassionate dialogue, they create a safe space where individuals feel heard and valued, paving the way for more meaningful relationships. This approach not only alleviates feelings of isolation but also empowers those navigating the complexities of bipolar disorder to express themselves openly, nurturing a sense of belonging that is essential for emotional well-being.

Beyond the Labels: Understanding the Spectrum of Bipolar Disorder

Understanding the different types of bipolar disorder and their impacts is crucial in facilitating compassionate communication. Each variation, from Bipolar I to Cyclothymia, presents unique challenges and experiences. By educating ourselves on these distinctions, caregivers and loved ones can tailor their conversations to be more empathetic and relevant. This understanding fosters an environment where feelings can be discussed without judgment, ultimately leading to more effective communication strategies. The ability to recognize the nuances of the disorder allows for deeper connections and a greater appreciation of the journey that individuals face, reinforcing that they are not alone in their struggles.

Beyond the Labels: Understanding the Spectrum of Bipolar Disorder

In moments of crisis, compassionate communication becomes even more vital. Knowing when to seek professional help is a critical skill for caregivers and friends. By maintaining open lines of communication, they can better identify warning signs and respond appropriately to emotional upheavals. Compassionate dialogue encourages individuals to express their needs without fear, ensuring that they feel supported during turbulent times. This proactive approach not only aids in crisis management but also fosters resilience, as individuals learn to articulate their experiences and seek help when necessary, reinforcing the importance of community and support.

Beyond the Labels: Understanding the Spectrum of Bipolar Disorder

The role of self-care cannot be overstated, particularly for caregivers of individuals with bipolar disorder. Engaging in compassionate communication not only benefits the individual but also allows caregivers to express their own feelings and boundaries. By sharing their experiences, they can cultivate a network of understanding and support among peers who face similar challenges. This mutual exchange of compassion can alleviate the emotional toll that caregiving often entails, reminding caregivers that they, too, deserve empathy and understanding. In this way, compassionate communication becomes a two-way street, where both parties can thrive.

Beyond the Labels: Understanding the Spectrum of Bipolar Disorder

Finally, building a support network rooted in compassionate communication enhances the overall experience for everyone involved. Friends, family, and professionals can collaborate to create an atmosphere of understanding, fostering an environment where individuals with bipolar disorder can flourish. Sharing personal stories and real-life experiences can bridge gaps in understanding, creating a tapestry of support that is both rich and diverse. By prioritizing compassionate dialogue, we cultivate a culture of empathy that not only benefits those with bipolar disorder but also enriches the lives of everyone who stands beside them, encouraging growth, healing, and connection in the face of adversity.

Beyond the Labels: Understanding the Spectrum of Bipolar Disorder

Chapter 2: The Spectrum of Bipolar Disorder

Types of Bipolar Disorder: A Comprehensive Guide

Bipolar disorder is a complex mental health condition that manifests in various forms, each with its unique characteristics and challenges. Understanding the different types of bipolar disorder is crucial for patients, families, and friends, as it lays the foundation for effective communication, empathy, and support. The most recognized forms include Bipolar I, Bipolar II, and Cyclothymic Disorder, each presenting distinct patterns of mood swings that can profoundly impact daily life. By gaining insight into these types, caregivers and loved ones can better tailor their approaches, fostering a nurturing environment conducive to healing and growth.

Beyond the Labels: Understanding the Spectrum of Bipolar Disorder

Bipolar I disorder is characterized by manic episodes that last at least seven days or by manic symptoms that are so severe that immediate hospital care is needed. Depressive episodes often occur as well, lasting at least two weeks. The intensity of the manic episodes can lead to significant disruptions in one's life, affecting relationships, work, and overall well-being. Recognizing the signs of mania and depression allows families and friends to intervene early, providing essential support during critical times. It's vital for loved ones to remain vigilant and compassionate, helping to navigate the often turbulent waters of this disorder.

Beyond the Labels: Understanding the Spectrum of Bipolar Disorder

Bipolar II disorder, on the other hand, involves a pattern of depressive episodes and hypomanic episodes, which are less severe than the full-blown mania seen in Bipolar I. Individuals with Bipolar II may experience periods of high energy and creativity but typically do not reach the extreme levels of mania. This type can often be misdiagnosed or overlooked, as the hypomanic phases can appear less disruptive. For families and caregivers, understanding this distinction is essential to validate the experiences of their loved ones and provide the appropriate support during depressive episodes, which can be debilitating.

Beyond the Labels: Understanding the Spectrum of Bipolar Disorder

Cyclothymic disorder is a milder form of bipolar disorder, marked by numerous periods of hypomanic symptoms and periods of depressive symptoms that last for at least two years in adults (one year in children and adolescents). While the mood swings are less severe than those seen in Bipolar I or II, they can still create challenges in maintaining stable relationships and achieving personal goals. Awareness of cyclothymic disorder can empower caregivers and friends to recognize that even subtle mood fluctuations deserve attention and empathy, reinforcing the importance of open communication and understanding.

Beyond the Labels: Understanding the Spectrum of Bipolar Disorder

In conclusion, recognizing the different types of bipolar disorder is not just a clinical exercise; it is a vital step toward fostering deeper connections and support systems. Each type presents unique challenges, but with knowledge and compassion, families and loved ones can navigate the emotional landscape more effectively. By sharing experiences, building supportive networks, and encouraging open dialogue, we can create an environment where individuals with bipolar disorder feel understood, valued, and empowered on their journey toward stability and fulfillment.

Recognizing the Impact on Individuals and Families

Recognizing the impact of bipolar disorder on individuals and their families is crucial for fostering understanding and compassion. When a loved one struggles with this condition, the emotional landscape can shift dramatically, creating challenges that ripple through family dynamics. It is essential to acknowledge the unique experiences of those affected by bipolar disorder, as well as the profound effects on family members, friends, and caregivers who share in the journey. Each individual's experience is distinct, but the common thread of navigating the complexities of this disorder binds families together in a shared narrative of resilience and hope.

Beyond the Labels: Understanding the Spectrum of Bipolar Disorder

For individuals living with bipolar disorder, the experience can be both isolating and overwhelming. Fluctuating moods, from the highs of mania to the depths of depression, may lead to feelings of confusion and despair. This emotional turbulence can strain relationships, making it difficult for loved ones to understand what their family member is going through. Open communication becomes a vital tool in bridging the gap between personal experience and external perception. Encouraging discussions about feelings, fears, and needs can foster a supportive environment where everyone feels heard and valued, which is essential in managing the disorder effectively.

Beyond the Labels: Understanding the Spectrum of Bipolar Disorder

Family members and friends often find themselves on an emotional rollercoaster as they navigate the ups and downs associated with bipolar disorder. It's important for them to recognize their own feelings, including frustration, sadness, or helplessness, and to seek support in coping with these emotions. Building a support network can be a game-changer; connecting with others who understand the challenges can provide comfort and practical advice. This network may include support groups, online forums, and professional resources, all of which contribute to a collective strength that empowers families to face the disorder together.

Beyond the Labels: Understanding the Spectrum of Bipolar Disorder

Caregivers play a pivotal role in the lives of those with bipolar disorder, often sacrificing their own well-being in the process. Self-care for caregivers is not just a luxury; it is a necessity. Engaging in activities that nourish the mind and body can significantly enhance their ability to provide care. This includes finding time for hobbies, exercising, and seeking therapy or counseling as needed. Recognizing one's limits and establishing boundaries can prevent burnout and ensure that caregivers remain healthy and resilient, ultimately benefiting both themselves and their loved ones.

Beyond the Labels: Understanding the Spectrum of Bipolar Disorder

As families navigate the complexities of bipolar disorder, sharing personal stories and experiences can serve as a powerful source of inspiration and strength. Each journey through the challenges posed by this disorder is unique, yet the collective wisdom gained from these experiences can guide others in similar situations. By embracing vulnerability and openness, families can create an atmosphere of support that fosters healing and growth. In doing so, they not only enrich their own lives but also contribute to a broader understanding of bipolar disorder, breaking down the stigma and encouraging a more compassionate dialogue around mental health.

Beyond the Labels: Understanding the Spectrum of Bipolar Disorder

<u>Real Life Story:</u>

"My wife had a manic episode where she wanted to quit her job and start a new career overnight. It was hard to stay calm, but I remembered her therapist's advice: don't argue. Instead, I said, 'Let's explore this idea together when you're feeling settled.' The next week, she thanked me for not pressuring her during her mania."

What I learned: Staying calm and validating feelings prevents conflict during episodes.

Mental health
Daily tracker

Date ___________________________

Mo   Tu   We   Th   Fr   Sa   Su

My sleep last night was

Approx. hours ___________________

Get up time ___________________

How am I feeling this morning?

Great   Good   Okay   Not good   Awful

Day to do list

- Brush teeth and wash face
- Open a window and get fresh air
- Get done work tasks
- Time off screens
- Eat breakfast and lunch
- Move my body or take a walk

Today I intend ___________________________

____

Eye exercises   1   2   3

Cups of water   1   2   3   4   5   6

Evening to do list

- Read 20 pages of a book
- Write to my journal
- Meditate for 10 minutes
- Workout for 30 minutes
- Brush teeth and wash face
- Take a shower

How am I feeling this evening?

Great   Good   Okay   Not good   Awful

Am I satisfied with this day?

I am grateful today for

____
____
____

What I like about myself today

____
____
____

What I managed to do today

____
____

What I would like to tell myself for tomorrow

Notes

How and what would I like to feel tomorrow

joy   appreciation   empowered   enthusiasm   fun   proud
strong   active   love   passion   freedom   happiness
optimism   belief   hope   inspired   courage   interest
amusement   gratitude   delight   relaxed   calm   confident
curious   focused   worthy   thrilled   self-respecting   kind

Chapter 3: Strategies for Effective Communication

Listening with Empathy

Listening with empathy is a transformative skill that can bridge the gap between understanding and support for those affected by bipolar disorder. When individuals living with this condition express their feelings, thoughts, and experiences, they often navigate a tumultuous emotional landscape. For family members, friends, and caregivers, taking the time to listen with genuine empathy can foster a deeper connection and create a safe space for open dialogue. This practice not only validates their feelings but also reinforces the notion that they are not alone in their journey.

Beyond the Labels: Understanding the Spectrum of Bipolar Disorder

Empathy involves more than just hearing words; it requires an active effort to understand the emotions behind those words. When we engage in empathetic listening, we tune into the nuances of tone, body language, and facial expressions. This attentiveness allows us to grasp the complexities of their experiences, whether they are experiencing highs or lows. By reflecting on their feelings and acknowledging their struggles without judgment, we can help reduce feelings of isolation and stigma often associated with bipolar disorder.

Incorporating empathetic listening into our interactions can also enhance the effectiveness of communication. Often, individuals with bipolar disorder may feel misunderstood or dismissed, leading to frustration and withdrawal. By practicing patience and allowing them the space to articulate their thoughts, we can encourage them to share more openly. This creates an opportunity for deeper conversations about their needs, fears, and hopes, fostering trust and strengthening relationships.

Beyond the Labels: Understanding the Spectrum of Bipolar Disorder

Beyond the Labels: Understanding the Spectrum of Bipolar Disorder

Furthermore, empathetic listening can serve as a vital tool during crisis situations. When emotions run high, the ability to listen without rushing to provide solutions can be transformative. Instead of trying to fix the problem immediately, we can focus on being present, offering a reassuring presence that conveys understanding and care. This approach not only calms the situation but also empowers individuals to express themselves more fully and seek the help they may need.

Ultimately, listening with empathy is an essential component of supporting loved ones with bipolar disorder. It encourages a culture of openness and acceptance, allowing individuals to feel valued and respected in their journey. As we cultivate this skill, we not only enhance our relationships but also contribute to a more compassionate environment for everyone affected by bipolar disorder. By embracing empathetic listening, we can inspire hope, resilience, and healing within ourselves and those we care about.

Expressing Yourself Clearly and Kindly

Expressing oneself clearly and kindly is a vital skill, particularly in the context of relationships involving individuals with bipolar disorder. Effective communication fosters understanding and connection, bridging gaps that may arise due to the complexities of the disorder. When family members, friends, and caregivers communicate with compassion and clarity, they create an environment where individuals with bipolar disorder feel safe, valued, and understood. This approach not only helps in managing day-to-day interactions but also strengthens the support system that is crucial for navigating the emotional ups and downs characteristic of the disorder.

Beyond the Labels: Understanding the Spectrum of Bipolar Disorder

To express oneself clearly, it is essential to choose words carefully and to articulate thoughts without ambiguity. This involves not only speaking plainly but also being mindful of the emotional tone conveyed. For instance, using "I" statements can be particularly effective. Instead of saying, "You never listen to me," one might say, "I feel unheard when I try to share my thoughts." This small shift can significantly reduce defensiveness and create an open dialogue, allowing for a more productive conversation. Encouraging open-ended questions also invites deeper discussions, fostering a connection that encourages individuals with bipolar disorder to share their feelings and experiences.

Beyond the Labels: Understanding the Spectrum of Bipolar Disorder

Kindness in communication goes hand in hand with clarity. Recognizing that individuals with bipolar disorder may experience heightened sensitivity during mood episodes is crucial. A gentle tone, patience, and a willingness to listen can make all the difference. When expressing concerns or discussing difficult topics, framing them in a supportive manner can help. For example, rather than criticizing a behavior, one might express concern by saying, "I'm worried about how you're feeling lately. How can I support you?" This approach not only validates their feelings but also reinforces the message that they are not alone in their struggles.

Beyond the Labels: Understanding the Spectrum of Bipolar Disorder

It is also important to be aware of non-verbal communication, as body language and facial expressions can significantly impact how messages are received. Maintaining an open posture, making eye contact, and using a calm voice can convey empathy and understanding. When discussing sensitive topics, creating a comfortable environment, free from distractions, can facilitate a more open exchange. Taking the time to ensure that both parties are in a good emotional space to communicate can lead to more meaningful interactions, paving the way for healing and connection.

Beyond the Labels: Understanding the Spectrum of Bipolar Disorder

Ultimately, expressing oneself clearly and kindly is an ongoing practice that benefits everyone involved. It invites collaboration, enhances understanding, and fosters resilience within relationships impacted by bipolar disorder. By prioritizing compassionate communication, we not only support our loved ones but also nurture our own emotional well-being. In the journey of living with bipolar disorder, every effort to communicate with clarity and kindness contributes to a more supportive and loving environment, making it a vital component of care for all involved.

REMINDER

Taking care of
yourself is
productive

Chapter 4: Self-Care for Caregivers

Prioritizing Your Own Well-Being

Prioritizing your own well-being is an essential yet often overlooked aspect of navigating life with or alongside bipolar disorder. Whether you are a patient, a family member, a friend, or a caregiver, it's crucial to recognize that your mental and emotional health directly impacts your ability to support others. Embracing self-care not only enhances your resilience but also fosters a healthier environment for those you care about. By taking the time to nurture your own needs, you create a foundation for more effective communication and deeper connections with loved ones.

Beyond the Labels: Understanding the Spectrum of Bipolar Disorder

Establishing boundaries is one of the first steps in prioritizing your well-being. It's easy to become overwhelmed when trying to support someone with bipolar disorder, especially during challenging times. Learning to say no when necessary and ensuring you have time for your own interests and relaxation can help prevent burnout. This doesn't mean you care any less; rather, it signifies a commitment to being the best version of yourself for others. Healthy boundaries allow you to recharge and maintain the emotional energy needed to provide support when it matters most.

Beyond the Labels: Understanding the Spectrum of Bipolar Disorder

Self-care practices can take many forms, from engaging in physical activities to pursuing creative outlets. It's important to identify what brings you joy and peace. Whether it's taking a nature walk, practicing mindfulness, or enjoying a favorite hobby, these moments are vital for replenishing your spirit. Surrounding yourself with positive influences, including friends and support groups, can also reinforce your commitment to self-care. Sharing experiences with others who understand the complexities of bipolar disorder can be both comforting and empowering, reminding you that you are not alone in your journey.

Beyond the Labels: Understanding the Spectrum of Bipolar Disorder

In times of crisis, your own well-being becomes even more critical. Being prepared to navigate these situations requires a calm and centered mindset. When you prioritize your mental health, you enhance your ability to respond effectively during emergencies. This might involve having a crisis plan in place or knowing when to seek professional help. By maintaining a focus on self-care, you equip yourself to be a stable presence, guiding your loved ones through their emotional rollercoasters while ensuring your own stability.

Ultimately, prioritizing your well-being is not an act of selfishness but rather a powerful affirmation of your commitment to those you love. By being a healthy, balanced individual, you create a ripple effect that positively impacts everyone around you. It's a journey of empowerment—one that not only enriches your life but also strengthens the bonds with your loved ones. Embrace self-care as a vital aspect of your life, and watch how it transforms your relationships and enhances your capacity to support others in their struggles with bipolar disorder.

Developing Healthy Coping Strategies

Developing healthy coping strategies is essential for individuals navigating the complexities of bipolar disorder, as well as for their families and friends. The emotional ups and downs associated with the condition can be overwhelming, but with the right tools, everyone involved can find balance and resilience. It's important to recognize that coping is a skill that can be cultivated over time, and it begins with understanding the unique challenges presented by bipolar disorder. This journey not only enhances the quality of life for those directly affected but also strengthens the bonds among family members and friends.

Beyond the Labels: Understanding the Spectrum of Bipolar Disorder

One critical aspect of developing healthy coping strategies is effective communication. Open and honest dialogue fosters understanding and creates a safe space for individuals experiencing mood fluctuations. Family members and friends should practice active listening, validating feelings without judgment. This approach helps in expressing support and encourages those with bipolar disorder to share their experiences. Furthermore, establishing clear boundaries is vital. It allows caregivers and loved ones to support without becoming overwhelmed, ensuring that everyone's emotional needs are met.

Self-care for caregivers cannot be overlooked. Those who support individuals with bipolar disorder often face emotional fatigue. Prioritizing personal well-being is crucial for maintaining a balanced and supportive environment. Engaging in activities that promote relaxation and joy, such as hobbies, exercise, or mindfulness practices, can significantly enhance one's capacity to care for others. By modeling healthy coping mechanisms, caregivers not only improve their own mental health but also provide a positive example for their loved ones, illustrating the importance of self-care in managing stress.

Beyond the Labels: Understanding the Spectrum of Bipolar Disorder

In moments of crisis, knowing when to seek professional help is a vital skill that can save lives. Families and friends should be educated about warning signs and symptoms that indicate an escalation in mood episodes. Having a clear plan in place, including emergency contacts and local mental health resources, empowers everyone to act decisively when necessary. This proactive approach not only alleviates anxiety but also reinforces a sense of security and support, showing that help is always available.

Beyond the Labels: Understanding the Spectrum of Bipolar Disorder

Building a strong support network is instrumental in fostering resilience for both individuals with bipolar disorder and their loved ones. Connecting with support groups, online communities, and educational resources can offer invaluable insights and shared experiences. This network not only provides emotional backing but also practical advice on navigating the challenges posed by bipolar disorder. As families and friends collaborate, they create a tapestry of support that uplifts everyone involved, transforming what may feel like an isolating journey into one filled with understanding, hope, and shared strength.

Chapter 5: Navigating Crisis Situations

Identifying Signs of Crisis

Identifying signs of crisis in individuals with bipolar disorder is crucial for fostering understanding and support within families and communities. A crisis may manifest as an escalation of symptoms, which can include intense mood swings, heightened irritability, or severe depressive episodes. Friends and family members often play a vital role in recognizing these changes, as they may be the first to observe shifts in behavior or mood that signal trouble. By being mindful of these signs, loved ones can take proactive steps toward intervention, ensuring that the individual receives the help they need before the situation escalates further.

Beyond the Labels: Understanding the Spectrum of Bipolar Disorder

It's essential to understand that the signs of crisis can vary widely among individuals with bipolar disorder. Some may exhibit extreme energy levels or engage in risky behaviors during manic episodes, while others may withdraw from social interactions or show signs of hopelessness during depressive phases. Educating oneself about the different types of bipolar disorder and their respective characteristics is key to recognizing these patterns. Family members and caregivers can become more attuned to the nuances of their loved ones' experiences, which can empower them to respond more effectively during challenging times.

Beyond the Labels: Understanding the Spectrum of Bipolar Disorder

Communication plays a fundamental role in identifying a crisis. Open dialogue can help individuals express their feelings and experiences, which may not always be visible to others. It is important for family members and friends to create a safe space where those with bipolar disorder feel comfortable sharing their thoughts. This can involve discussing feelings without judgment and being willing to listen actively. Encouraging open conversations about mental health can lead to early recognition of distress, allowing for timely support and intervention.

In situations where signs of crisis are apparent, it's crucial to know when to seek professional help. This can be a daunting decision for families, but recognizing that reaching out is a sign of strength can alleviate some of the fear associated with intervention. Whether it involves contacting a therapist, a psychiatrist, or a crisis hotline, understanding the resources available can make a significant difference. Families and caregivers should be equipped with knowledge about local mental health services, ensuring they can act swiftly when the need arises.

Beyond the Labels: Understanding the Spectrum of Bipolar Disorder

Building a robust support network is also essential for navigating the complexities of bipolar disorder. This network can include family members, friends, mental health professionals, and support groups. Sharing personal stories and experiences can foster a sense of unity and understanding, reminding individuals that they are not alone in their struggles. By actively participating in this supportive community, families and friends can enhance their coping mechanisms and resilience, ultimately contributing to a more stable and nurturing environment for their loved ones. Together, they can transform challenges into opportunities for growth, healing, and deeper connections.

When and How to Seek Help

Recognizing when to seek help can be a pivotal moment in the journey of living with bipolar disorder. It's essential to understand that both patients and their loved ones can experience overwhelming emotions and challenges. Whether it's a sudden change in mood, increased irritability, or an inability to cope with daily activities, these signs often indicate that professional intervention may be necessary. Seeking help is not a sign of weakness; rather, it demonstrates a commitment to well-being and a proactive approach to managing the disorder. Emphasizing open communication can empower individuals to express their feelings and concerns, making it easier to identify when additional support is needed.

Beyond the Labels: Understanding the Spectrum of Bipolar Disorder

There are various avenues to explore when seeking help. For individuals with bipolar disorder, the first step might involve reaching out to a trusted mental health professional, such as a psychologist or psychiatrist, who specializes in mood disorders. Family members or caregivers can also play a vital role by encouraging their loved ones to attend therapy sessions, support groups, or engage in psychiatric evaluations. Additionally, resources such as hotlines or community mental health centers can provide immediate support and guidance. By fostering a collaborative approach, families can ensure that the individual feels supported and understood throughout the process.

Beyond the Labels: Understanding the Spectrum of Bipolar Disorder

In moments of crisis, knowing how to navigate the situation is crucial. Families should establish a clear plan of action for emergencies, which may include identifying local mental health resources and understanding the signs that warrant immediate professional help. This could be a significant escalation in mood swings, thoughts of self-harm, or any behavior that puts the individual or others at risk. By preparing ahead of time, families can reduce panic and create a safer environment where their loved one can receive the help they need without delay.

Beyond the Labels: Understanding the Spectrum of Bipolar Disorder

Support networks are invaluable in this journey of managing bipolar disorder. Building a strong support system that includes family, friends, and mental health professionals can offer a sense of belonging and reassurance. Such networks can provide emotional support, share coping strategies, and even participate in educational workshops to better understand the nuances of the disorder. Encouraging family members and friends to connect with local or online support groups can also facilitate the sharing of experiences and resources, ultimately strengthening the collective resilience of everyone involved.

Beyond the Labels: Understanding the Spectrum of Bipolar Disorder

The role of self-care cannot be overstated for both individuals with bipolar disorder and their support networks. Caregivers must prioritize their mental and physical well-being to effectively support their loved ones. This may involve setting healthy boundaries, engaging in stress-reducing activities, and actively seeking their own support systems. By practicing self-care, caregivers not only safeguard their own health but also enhance their capacity to provide compassionate, informed support to those they care for. Ultimately, seeking help is a courageous step toward healing and growth, fostering deeper connections and understanding within families and communities navigating the complexities of bipolar disorder.

Beyond the Labels: Understanding the Spectrum of Bipolar Disorder

Beyond the Labels: Understanding the Spectrum of Bipolar Disorder

Chapter 6: Building a Support Network

Connecting with Resources and Organizations

Connecting with resources and organizations that specialize in bipolar disorder is a vital step for patients, families, and caregivers alike. These resources provide essential information, support networks, and a sense of community for those navigating the complexities of this mental health condition. Organizations such as the National Alliance on Mental Illness (NAMI) and the Depression and Bipolar Support Alliance (DBSA) offer invaluable tools, including hotlines, educational materials, and peer support groups. Engaging with these organizations can empower individuals to better understand the nuances of bipolar disorder and foster meaningful connections with others who share similar experiences.

Beyond the Labels: Understanding the Spectrum of Bipolar Disorder

Establishing a support network is crucial for anyone affected by bipolar disorder. This network can include mental health professionals, support groups, and even online communities. By reaching out to others, individuals can share strategies for effective communication, learn about the different types of bipolar disorder, and explore coping mechanisms that have worked for others. These interactions can help normalize the emotional rollercoaster that often accompanies the condition, providing comfort and understanding to both patients and their loved ones. The collective wisdom of a support network can be a powerful tool in managing relationships, balancing boundaries, and offering support.

Beyond the Labels: Understanding the Spectrum of Bipolar Disorder

For caregivers, self-care is paramount. Connecting with resources that focus on caregiver well-being can lead to more effective support for those with bipolar disorder. Organizations often provide workshops, educational materials, and online forums where caregivers can share their experiences and learn from one another. Understanding the importance of self-care allows caregivers to recharge and maintain their own mental health, ultimately benefiting the individuals they care for. This reciprocal relationship highlights the importance of seeking out support systems that prioritize caregiver needs alongside those of the patient.

Beyond the Labels: Understanding the Spectrum of Bipolar Disorder

Navigating crisis situations can be daunting, and knowing when to seek professional help is essential. Many organizations offer crisis intervention resources and training programs to help families recognize warning signs and respond effectively. These resources can empower families to act swiftly in times of need, ensuring that their loved ones receive the support they require. Organizations often provide education on effective crisis management techniques, which can alleviate the anxiety surrounding these situations and foster a sense of preparedness and resilience.

Beyond the Labels: Understanding the Spectrum of Bipolar Disorder

Finally, sharing personal stories within these networks can be profoundly inspiring. Real-life experiences of supporting loved ones with bipolar disorder can serve as a beacon of hope for those currently struggling. By connecting with others who have walked a similar path, individuals can gain insights into effective strategies, emotional coping mechanisms, and the transformative power of community. The bond formed through shared experiences can create a supportive environment where everyone feels understood and less isolated, ultimately reinforcing the message that no one is alone in their journey with bipolar disorder.

The Power of Community Support

Community support plays a vital role in the lives of those affected by bipolar disorder, fostering an environment where understanding and compassion thrive. Individuals navigating the complexities of this condition often feel isolated, grappling with the stigma that surrounds mental health issues. However, when a community comes together, it cultivates a sense of belonging that can alleviate feelings of loneliness and despair. Friends, family, and support groups can create a network of encouragement that empowers individuals to share their experiences, seek help, and embrace their journey with bipolar disorder.

Beyond the Labels: Understanding the Spectrum of Bipolar Disorder

Effective communication is the cornerstone of community support. By fostering open dialogues, loved ones can better understand the unique challenges faced by individuals with bipolar disorder. Active listening, empathy, and validation are essential components of these conversations. When family members and friends take the time to learn about the different types of bipolar disorder and their impacts, they can engage more meaningfully. This knowledge equips them to approach discussions with sensitivity and care, ensuring that the person feels heard and respected. Creating a safe space for sharing emotions can lead to deeper connections and a stronger support network.

Beyond the Labels: Understanding the Spectrum of Bipolar Disorder

Self-care for caregivers is equally important in this dynamic. Those who support individuals with bipolar disorder often experience emotional fatigue and stress. Building a robust community means recognizing the needs of caregivers and providing them with the resources to recharge. This could involve establishing support groups specifically for caregivers, emphasizing the importance of their mental health. When caregivers prioritize their well-being, they become more effective in their roles, which ultimately benefits the individuals they support. Encouragement to seek respite, engage in hobbies, and connect with others can transform the caregiving experience into a more balanced and fulfilling journey.

Navigating crisis situations is another area where community support shines. During challenging times, knowing when to seek professional help is crucial, and a supportive network can help identify these moments. Friends and family can act as a safety net, providing insight and guidance from their observations. By being educated on the signs of crisis, community members can step in when necessary, ensuring the individual receives timely assistance. This proactive approach fosters a culture of care where seeking help is seen as a strength rather than a weakness, reinforcing the idea that no one has to face their struggles alone.

Beyond the Labels: Understanding the Spectrum of Bipolar Disorder

Ultimately, the power of community support lies in its ability to transform lives. By sharing personal stories and real-life experiences, individuals can inspire hope and resilience within their communities. These narratives not only highlight the challenges faced but also celebrate the triumphs of individuals living with bipolar disorder. As community members rally together, they create an atmosphere where recovery is possible, and every voice matters. Through connection, understanding, and shared experiences, the journey through bipolar disorder can become less daunting, paving the way for healing and growth.

Beyond the Labels: Understanding the Spectrum of Bipolar Disorder

7 Days Of Journal Prompts

Monday
What are 10 words that describe your personality?

Tuesday
What are 5 of your boundaries?

Wednesday
What are 10 things you're passionate about?

Thursday
What are 5 of your unique superpowers?

Friday
What are 3 things you'd like to improve about yourself?

Saturday
What are 5 qualities you admire in other people?

Sunday
What are 3 new things you'd like to try or learn more about?

Chapter 7: Managing Relationships

Setting Boundaries with Love

Setting boundaries with love is essential for fostering healthy relationships when navigating the complexities of bipolar disorder. It is a delicate balance; boundaries protect both the individual with bipolar disorder and their loved ones, while love ensures that these boundaries are set with compassion and understanding. By establishing clear parameters, family members, friends, and caregivers can create an environment that promotes stability and respect, enabling everyone involved to feel safe and valued.

Beyond the Labels: Understanding the Spectrum of Bipolar Disorder

Effective communication plays a pivotal role in setting boundaries. Open dialogues about needs and limitations can prevent misunderstandings and resentment. It is crucial to approach these conversations with empathy, recognizing that the person with bipolar disorder may have fluctuating emotional states. Using "I" statements can help express feelings without placing blame, such as "I feel overwhelmed when..." This gentle approach encourages the individual to understand the impact of their actions while reinforcing the importance of mutual respect in the relationship.

Understanding the different types of bipolar disorder and their unique challenges can further enhance boundary-setting efforts. Each type can manifest in various ways, impacting emotions, behaviors, and interactions. By educating themselves about the specific nuances, family members and friends can tailor their boundaries to suit the individual's condition. This knowledge fosters patience and compassion, enabling loved ones to navigate the emotional landscape with greater insight and care, ultimately strengthening the bond they share.

Beyond the Labels: Understanding the Spectrum of Bipolar Disorder

Self-care is equally important for caregivers and family members. Establishing boundaries does not only protect the individual with bipolar disorder but also safeguards the mental and emotional well-being of those offering support. Caregivers must remember that their needs are valid and deserving of attention. By incorporating self-care practices into their routines, they can recharge and approach their loved ones from a place of strength and resilience. This self-awareness can prevent burnout and enhance the quality of support provided to the individual.

Beyond the Labels: Understanding the Spectrum of Bipolar Disorder

Building a support network is vital in this journey. Engaging with other families and friends who share similar experiences can provide comfort and understanding. Sharing personal stories and coping strategies fosters a sense of community, reminding caregivers that they are not alone in their struggles. As they navigate the complexities of bipolar disorder together, they can learn from one another, refining their approaches to boundary-setting with love and compassion, ultimately enriching their relationships and creating a more supportive environment for everyone involved.

Offering Support Without Losing Yourself

Offering support to someone with bipolar disorder can be both a rewarding and challenging endeavor. It's essential to remember that while your presence and assistance can make a significant difference, it is equally important to maintain your own well-being. Supporting a loved one involves emotional investment, and without proper boundaries and self-care, you risk becoming overwhelmed. The journey of offering support is not just about standing strong for others; it requires a mindful approach to ensure that you do not lose yourself in the process.

Beyond the Labels: Understanding the Spectrum of Bipolar Disorder

Establishing clear boundaries is a foundational step in maintaining your identity while providing support. This means recognizing your limits and communicating them effectively. When you set boundaries, you create a safe space for both you and your loved one. It allows you to engage in meaningful conversations without feeling drained or resentful. Remember, your role is to support, not to fix. By acknowledging that you cannot control their experiences or emotions, you empower both yourself and the individual you care for to seek the help they need without placing undue pressure on your relationship.

Beyond the Labels: Understanding the Spectrum of Bipolar Disorder

Self-care is not a luxury; it is a necessity for anyone supporting a person with bipolar disorder. Just as you encourage your loved one to prioritize their mental health, you must do the same for yourself. Engage in activities that rejuvenate your spirit, whether it's pursuing hobbies, spending time with friends, or simply taking a moment to breathe. By taking care of your own mental and emotional needs, you equip yourself to be a more effective supporter. This balance fosters resilience and patience, qualities that are invaluable during difficult times.

Effective communication is also vital in the support process. Approach interactions with empathy and openness, allowing space for your loved one to express their feelings without fear of judgment. Listen actively and validate their experiences, ensuring they feel heard and understood. This creates a strong foundation of trust and respect, which can significantly enhance your relationship. However, be mindful of not absorbing their emotions as your own; instead, practice reflective listening, which allows you to engage while maintaining your emotional distance.

Beyond the Labels: Understanding the Spectrum of Bipolar Disorder

Lastly, don't hesitate to seek help for yourself when needed. Just as your loved one may require professional guidance, you too can benefit from counseling or support groups. Sharing your experiences with others who understand the complexities of living with or supporting someone with bipolar disorder can provide comfort and insight. Remember, you are not alone in this journey. By embracing your needs alongside those of your loved one, you can cultivate a healthier, more supportive environment that benefits everyone involved. Together, with compassion and understanding, you can navigate the challenges of bipolar disorder while preserving your own identity and well-being.

Chapter 8: The Role of Therapy and Medication

Understanding Treatment Options

Navigating the landscape of bipolar disorder treatment can be daunting, but embracing the available options empowers patients and their support systems. Treatment for bipolar disorder is not a one-size-fits-all approach; it is as unique as each individual. Patients may benefit from a combination of medication, therapy, and lifestyle changes that collectively promote stability and well-being. By understanding these diverse treatment options, patients, families, and caregivers can work collaboratively to create tailored strategies that resonate with their specific needs.

Beyond the Labels: Understanding the Spectrum of Bipolar Disorder

Medication plays a crucial role in managing bipolar disorder, often helping to stabilize mood fluctuations and enhance quality of life. Mood stabilizers, antipsychotics, and antidepressants are among the common medications prescribed, each serving a specific purpose in the treatment plan. It's essential for patients to maintain open communication with their healthcare providers to find the right balance of medications. Adjustments may be necessary over time, and being proactive about side effects or concerns can significantly influence the effectiveness of the treatment regimen.

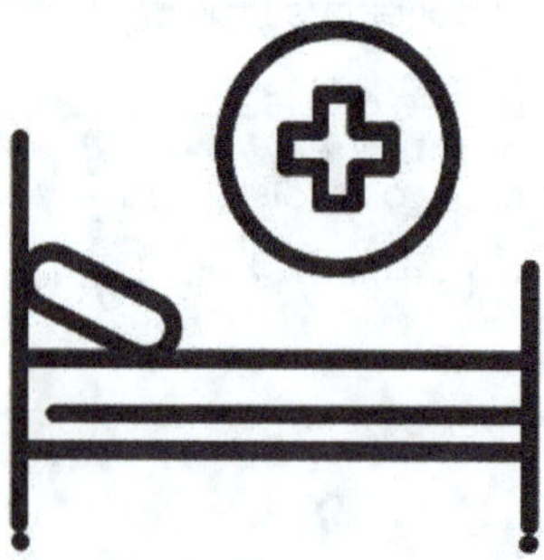

Beyond the Labels: Understanding the Spectrum of Bipolar Disorder

Therapy offers an invaluable complement to medication. Various therapeutic modalities, including cognitive-behavioral therapy (CBT), interpersonal therapy, and family-focused therapy, can equip patients and their loved ones with tools to navigate challenges. These therapies foster understanding and facilitate effective communication, which is vital in managing relationships during the highs and lows of bipolar disorder. Regular therapy sessions provide a safe space for expressing emotions, exploring triggers, and developing coping strategies, thereby enhancing the overall treatment experience.

Beyond the Labels: Understanding the Spectrum of Bipolar Disorder

Self-care is another fundamental aspect of managing bipolar disorder. For patients, this might involve establishing a daily routine, focusing on nutrition, exercising regularly, and practicing mindfulness. For caregivers and family members, self-care is equally important to prevent burnout and maintain their own mental health. Engaging in supportive communities, seeking respite care, and prioritizing personal interests can help caregivers recharge, ultimately benefiting both themselves and their loved ones. Understanding that caring for oneself is not selfish, but rather a vital part of the caregiving journey, can foster resilience.

Beyond the Labels: Understanding the Spectrum of Bipolar Disorder

Building a strong support network is essential in navigating the complexities of bipolar disorder. Involvement in support groups, educational workshops, and community resources can provide invaluable insights and encouragement. Family and friends play an integral role in this network, offering emotional support and understanding. By educating themselves about bipolar disorder, loved ones can better manage their own feelings and provide informed support. Sharing personal experiences and strategies within this circle can create a foundation of strength, fostering an environment where everyone feels valued and empowered in their journey together.

The Benefits of a Collaborative Approach

A collaborative approach to managing bipolar disorder can serve as a powerful catalyst for healing and understanding within families and support networks. This method emphasizes open communication, mutual respect, and shared decision-making between individuals with bipolar disorder and their loved ones. By fostering an environment in which everyone feels valued and heard, families can create a foundation of trust that encourages open dialogue about feelings, triggers, and experiences. This not only helps in coping with the challenges of the disorder but also strengthens the bonds between family members, promoting a sense of unity in the face of adversity.

Beyond the Labels: Understanding the Spectrum of Bipolar Disorder

One of the most significant benefits of collaboration is the opportunity to understand the spectrum of bipolar disorder more thoroughly. Each person experiences the condition differently, and through collective discussions, families can gain insights into the specific needs and challenges of their loved one. This understanding enables caregivers and family members to better tailor their support strategies, whether that involves adjusting communication styles, recognizing early warning signs of mood changes, or providing appropriate emotional support. An informed approach can lead to more effective management of the disorder, ultimately fostering a more harmonious home environment.

Beyond the Labels: Understanding the Spectrum of Bipolar Disorder

Collaboration also allows for the sharing of coping strategies among family members and friends. By pooling resources and experiences, families can identify practical methods that work well for everyone involved. For instance, caregivers can exchange self-care techniques that help them recharge and maintain their well-being while supporting their loved one. In this way, the emotional burden does not solely rest on one individual, reducing feelings of isolation and resentment that can arise in caregiving situations. When everyone contributes to the conversation, the collective wisdom can lead to innovative solutions that might not have been discovered in a more isolated approach.

Beyond the Labels: Understanding the Spectrum of Bipolar Disorder

Moreover, a collaborative approach helps to establish clear boundaries and expectations, which are crucial for maintaining healthy relationships. By openly discussing needs and limitations, family members can create a framework that ensures everyone feels safe and respected. This is especially important in navigating the emotional rollercoasters that often accompany bipolar disorder, as it allows individuals to articulate when they need space or support. Setting these boundaries not only protects the well-being of the caregiver but also empowers the person with bipolar disorder to take ownership of their journey, fostering independence and resilience.

Beyond the Labels: Understanding the Spectrum of Bipolar Disorder

Finally, embracing a collaborative mindset can turn the management of bipolar disorder into a shared journey rather than a solitary battle. This sense of togetherness can be profoundly uplifting, transforming challenges into opportunities for growth and connection. By engaging in joint problem-solving, families can celebrate victories—both big and small—together, reinforcing the notion that they are not alone in this journey. Ultimately, a collaborative approach nurtures hope, resilience, and understanding, making it an invaluable strategy for anyone touched by bipolar disorder.

My Safety Plan

Remember: Help is always available.

1.My warning signs are:	2. My effective coping strategies are:
*These can be thoughts, feelings or behaviors that indicate you are at risk.	*These are things you can do to help lift your mood, like meditation or exercise.
3. People I can reach out to for distraction:	4. People I can reach out to for help:
Person 1: Contact No.	Person 1: Contact No.
Person 2: Contact No.	Person 2: Contact No.
Person 3: Contact No.	Person 3: Contact No.
5. Steps I can take to make my environment safer:	6. In the event of a crisis:
Please List 1 2. 3. 4.	Call Emergency Contact #1: Call Crisis Hotline. Call Emergency Services:

Chapter 9: Coping Mechanisms for Families

Embracing the Emotional Rollercoaster

Embracing the emotional rollercoaster of bipolar disorder requires a profound understanding of the fluctuations that characterize this condition. Individuals with bipolar disorder experience intense highs, known as mania or hypomania, alongside deep lows, or depressive episodes. For families, friends, and caregivers, recognizing these emotional shifts is essential for fostering a supportive environment. This journey is not merely about weathering the storms; it's about learning to dance in the rain, celebrating the small victories, and navigating the complexities with compassion and resilience.

Beyond the Labels: Understanding the Spectrum of Bipolar Disorder

Communication plays a pivotal role in managing the emotional ups and downs associated with bipolar disorder. Open and empathetic dialogue can bridge the gap between the experiences of those living with the disorder and their loved ones. Encouraging individuals to share their feelings during both manic and depressive phases fosters a deeper connection and understanding. It is crucial to listen without judgment, validate their experiences, and express unconditional support. By creating a safe space for honest conversations, families can help their loved ones feel seen and heard, making the emotional journey a shared experience rather than a solitary one.

Beyond the Labels: Understanding the Spectrum of Bipolar Disorder

Self-care for caregivers is equally important in this emotional landscape. Supporting someone with bipolar disorder can be taxing, and caregivers must prioritize their own mental and emotional well-being to remain effective advocates. Establishing healthy boundaries, seeking support from peers, and engaging in activities that bring joy can mitigate feelings of stress and overwhelm. Caregivers should acknowledge their own emotional fluctuations and practice self-compassion, recognizing that it's okay to seek help and take breaks when needed. By nurturing themselves, caregivers can better support their loved ones through the highs and lows of the disorder.

Beyond the Labels: Understanding the Spectrum of Bipolar Disorder

Building a robust support network is vital for everyone involved. Family members and friends should connect with others who understand the challenges of living with bipolar disorder. Support groups, both in-person and online, provide valuable resources, encouragement, and shared experiences. These communities can help individuals feel less isolated in their struggles, offering insights and coping strategies that have worked for others. The emotional rollercoaster becomes more manageable when surrounded by a network of understanding, allowing everyone to share their experiences and learn from one another.

Beyond the Labels: Understanding the Spectrum of Bipolar Disorder

Ultimately, embracing the emotional rollercoaster of bipolar disorder is about fostering resilience and hope. Therapy and medication can provide essential tools for managing the disorder, but the journey involves every aspect of life. By focusing on effective communication, self-care, and community support, families and friends can build a foundation of stability and love. Sharing personal stories and experiences can illuminate the path forward, inspiring others to navigate their own journeys with courage. In this shared journey, every individual's story adds richness to understanding and acceptance, transforming the emotional highs and lows into a tapestry of connection and resilience.

Practical Strategies for Resilience

Resilience in the face of bipolar disorder is not just a personal journey; it is a shared voyage that involves loved ones, caregivers, and the broader support network. To cultivate resilience, effective communication stands at the forefront. Engaging in open, honest dialogue enables both the individual and their support system to express feelings, concerns, and aspirations. Practicing active listening, where each party focuses on understanding rather than responding, fosters a nurturing environment. Establishing regular check-ins can create a safe space for discussing challenges and triumphs, allowing everyone involved to feel heard and valued. This cultivates a sense of belonging and connection, which is vital for resilience.

Beyond the Labels: Understanding the Spectrum of Bipolar Disorder

Understanding the different types of bipolar disorder and their unique impacts is crucial for resilience. Knowledge empowers those affected to recognize patterns, triggers, and symptoms. Families and friends equipped with this understanding can anticipate challenges and respond appropriately, reducing feelings of helplessness. Educational resources such as workshops, books, and online forums can be invaluable tools. By learning together, families can create a collective understanding that not only enhances their ability to support but also strengthens their bonds. This shared knowledge can transform fear into action, enabling everyone to navigate the complexities of bipolar disorder with greater confidence.

Beyond the Labels: Understanding the Spectrum of Bipolar Disorder

Self-care for caregivers is another essential component of resilience. The emotional and physical toll of supporting someone with bipolar disorder can be significant. Caregivers must prioritize their own well-being, recognizing that a healthy caregiver is better equipped to provide support. Regular self-care routines, whether through exercise, hobbies, or simply taking time to recharge, can help maintain balance. Encouraging caregivers to seek support from peers, whether through support groups or one-on-one conversations, can alleviate feelings of isolation. By investing in their own health, caregivers can sustain their energy and compassion, which ultimately benefits the person they are supporting.

Navigating crisis situations requires a clear understanding of when professional help is necessary. Developing a crisis plan ahead of time can be invaluable, outlining specific steps to take and resources to contact. This proactive approach reduces panic during high-stress moments, allowing families to act decisively. Training in crisis intervention techniques can also empower loved ones to manage difficult situations effectively. By knowing what to do and whom to call, families can create a safety net that enhances resilience and ensures that the individual's needs are met promptly and compassionately.

Beyond the Labels: Understanding the Spectrum of Bipolar Disorder

Building a robust support network is essential for everyone involved. Connecting with local mental health organizations, online communities, and educational workshops can provide resources and support. These networks not only offer practical tools but also foster connections with others who understand the unique challenges of living with bipolar disorder. Sharing personal stories and experiences can be a powerful way to foster empathy and understanding, reminding everyone that they are not alone in their journey. Through collaboration and mutual support, resilience can flourish, transforming the challenges of bipolar disorder into opportunities for growth and connection.

Chapter 10: Educational Tools for Children and Teens

Helping Young Minds Understand Bipolar Disorder

Helping young minds understand bipolar disorder is essential in fostering empathy, reducing stigma, and building supportive environments. Children and adolescents often struggle with complex emotions and behaviors, especially when those around them are affected by mental health conditions. By providing age-appropriate information, we can empower young individuals to comprehend bipolar disorder's nuances, allowing them to navigate their relationships with affected family members or friends with compassion and understanding.

Beyond the Labels: Understanding the Spectrum of Bipolar Disorder

Education about bipolar disorder should begin with an emphasis on its nature as a medical condition, rather than a personal failing or a reason for shame. Explaining the different types of bipolar disorder—such as Bipolar I, Bipolar II, and Cyclothymic Disorder—can help young minds recognize that the disorder manifests in various ways. Using relatable examples and clear language can demystify the symptoms, such as mood swings, irritability, and changes in energy levels, allowing them to connect these experiences to their loved ones, fostering empathy rather than fear.

Beyond the Labels: Understanding the Spectrum of Bipolar Disorder

Incorporating discussions about emotional regulation can equip young individuals with vital tools to handle their feelings and reactions. Teaching them about the importance of self-care and healthy coping mechanisms can empower them to maintain their well-being while supporting someone with bipolar disorder. Encouraging practices such as mindfulness, journaling, and open communication can help them express their feelings and concerns in a constructive manner, ensuring that they feel heard and valued in their relationships.

Building a support network is crucial for both the individual affected by bipolar disorder and their loved ones. Young minds should be encouraged to seek out resources, whether through school counselors, support groups, or trusted adults. By understanding that they are not alone in their experiences, they can foster connections with others who share similar challenges. These relationships can provide a sense of belonging and reassurance, reinforcing that it is okay to ask for help when needed.

Finally, cultivating an atmosphere of openness about mental health can lead to healthier family dynamics. Sharing personal stories and experiences can bridge understanding and reinforce the message that mental health issues affect everyone in the family. By actively involving young individuals in conversations about bipolar disorder, we can create a generation that is not only informed but also compassionate, ultimately breaking down barriers and building a supportive community for those navigating the complexities of this condition.

Resources for Parents and Caregivers

In the journey of understanding and supporting loved ones with bipolar disorder, parents and caregivers can benefit immensely from a variety of resources designed to enhance their knowledge and skills. Books, articles, and online platforms dedicated to mental health can serve as valuable guides, providing insights into the complexities of bipolar disorder. Familiarizing oneself with the different types of bipolar disorder, including bipolar I, bipolar II, and cyclothymic disorder, can help caregivers recognize the unique challenges each individual may face. By equipping themselves with this knowledge, parents and caregivers can foster more effective communication and demonstrate empathy, ultimately strengthening their relationships with their loved ones.

Beyond the Labels: Understanding the Spectrum of Bipolar Disorder

In addition to literature, support groups can play a vital role in the emotional well-being of parents and caregivers. Connecting with others who share similar experiences can provide a sense of community and understanding that is often hard to find elsewhere. These groups offer a safe space for individuals to share their feelings, learn from each other's experiences, and find comfort in knowing they are not alone. Many organizations provide online forums and in-person meetings where caregivers can exchange coping strategies, discuss challenges, and celebrate victories. This collective support can empower parents and caregivers, reminding them that they are part of a larger network of individuals who truly understand the emotional rollercoaster of living with bipolar disorder.

Beyond the Labels: Understanding the Spectrum of Bipolar Disorder

Self-care is an essential aspect of supporting a loved one with bipolar disorder, yet it is often overlooked. Parents and caregivers must prioritize their own mental health and well-being to effectively provide support. Resources such as mindfulness practices, stress management techniques, and physical fitness programs can help caregivers recharge and maintain their resilience. Additionally, workshops and seminars focused on self-care can equip caregivers with practical tools to manage their stress and emotional fatigue. By investing time in their own health, caregivers not only nurture their well-being but also model the importance of self-care to their loved ones.

Beyond the Labels: Understanding the Spectrum of Bipolar Disorder

Navigating crisis situations can be daunting, making it crucial for parents and caregivers to know when to seek professional help. Resources such as crisis hotlines, mental health professionals, and emergency services can provide immediate support during challenging times. Understanding the warning signs of a crisis and having a plan in place can alleviate some of the fear and uncertainty that often accompany these situations. Parents and caregivers should familiarize themselves with local mental health resources, ensuring they have access to the right support when it matters most. This proactive approach can empower families to act confidently when crises arise, reinforcing their commitment to their loved one's safety and well-being.

Beyond the Labels: Understanding the Spectrum of Bipolar Disorder

Finally, building a robust support network is essential for families and friends of individuals with bipolar disorder. Engaging with professionals in non-medical roles, such as social workers, educators, and community leaders, can create a more comprehensive support system. Educational tools and resources tailored for children and teens within the family can also foster understanding and acceptance, helping younger family members navigate their emotions. Sharing personal stories of triumphs and challenges can inspire hope and resilience, reminding everyone involved that while the journey may be difficult, there is strength in community and love. By embracing these resources, parents and caregivers can cultivate a nurturing environment that promotes healing and understanding for everyone affected by bipolar disorder.

Chapter 11: Sharing Personal Stories

Inspiring Narratives of Support and Love

In the journey through bipolar disorder, the narratives of support and love serve as powerful reminders of resilience and connection. Many individuals facing the challenges of bipolar disorder find solace in the stories of those who have stood by them, offering unwavering support during tumultuous times. These narratives highlight the profound impact that empathy, understanding, and patience can have on the lives of both patients and their loved ones. They illustrate that, even amidst the emotional rollercoasters, there exists a deep well of love that can provide strength and comfort.

Beyond the Labels: Understanding the Spectrum of Bipolar Disorder

One poignant story involves a mother who learned to navigate her daughter's mood swings not with frustration, but with compassion. She discovered the importance of listening without judgment, recognizing the need for her daughter to express herself freely during manic and depressive episodes. Through her willingness to understand the nuances of bipolar disorder, she cultivated an environment that fostered open communication. This narrative exemplifies how love can blossom when family members take the time to educate themselves about the disorder, ultimately leading to a more harmonious relationship.

Friends and siblings also play crucial roles in these inspiring narratives. A brother shared how he learned to balance his protective instincts with respect for his sister's autonomy. By establishing healthy boundaries while offering unconditional support, he became a pillar of strength during her darkest moments. His story serves as a testament to the fact that love is not only about being present but also about empowering loved ones to seek help and engage in their own healing journeys. These relationships remind us that every small act of kindness can have a ripple effect, creating a network of support that nurtures hope.

Beyond the Labels: Understanding the Spectrum of Bipolar Disorder

Caregivers, too, have their own narratives of inspiration. One caregiver recounted her experience of feeling overwhelmed yet finding solace in community support groups. Through sharing her challenges and triumphs with others in similar situations, she discovered the strength that comes from vulnerability. This collective sharing of experiences not only provided practical strategies for self-care but also reinforced the notion that no one is alone in their struggles. Such stories highlight the importance of building a robust support network, where caregivers can find resources, encouragement, and, most importantly, love.

Beyond the Labels: Understanding the Spectrum of Bipolar Disorder

Ultimately, the narratives of support and love woven throughout the experiences of those affected by bipolar disorder create a tapestry of hope and healing. They remind us that while the journey may be fraught with difficulties, it is also filled with moments of profound connection and understanding. These stories inspire individuals to seek knowledge, foster communication, and build supportive relationships, all of which are essential in navigating the complexities of bipolar disorder. In sharing these narratives, we illuminate the path toward a more compassionate world, where love and support are at the forefront of the mental health conversation.

Lessons Learned from Real-Life Experiences

Real-life experiences provide invaluable lessons for those navigating the complexities of bipolar disorder, whether as patients, family members, or caregivers. One of the most profound insights is the power of open communication. Families who foster an environment where emotions can be freely expressed often find that misunderstandings diminish. Patients thrive when loved ones actively listen and validate their feelings, creating a safe space that encourages sharing without judgment. By prioritizing dialogue, relationships can deepen, paving the way for mutual understanding and support.

Beyond the Labels: Understanding the Spectrum of Bipolar Disorder

Another critical lesson arises from recognizing the diverse manifestations of bipolar disorder. Each individual's experience is unique, shaped by their specific type of bipolar disorder, personal history, and social context. Family members and caregivers must educate themselves about these differences to tailor their support effectively. Understanding that mood swings may not only be about the disorder but also influenced by external factors such as stress or fatigue can lead to more compassionate responses and better strategies for managing challenging situations together.

Beyond the Labels: Understanding the Spectrum of Bipolar Disorder

Self-care for caregivers cannot be overlooked. The emotional toll of supporting someone with bipolar disorder can be profound. Caregivers often feel overwhelmed, and neglecting their own well-being can lead to burnout. Real-life experiences underscore the importance of establishing boundaries and engaging in self-care practices. This may include seeking support from peer groups, pursuing hobbies, or simply taking time for oneself. By prioritizing their mental health, caregivers can sustain their ability to provide effective support, ensuring they are present for their loved ones when it matters most.

Beyond the Labels: Understanding the Spectrum of Bipolar Disorder

Navigating crisis situations is another area where lessons are often learned through experience. Knowing when to seek professional help can be a daunting task, particularly for those who wish to manage without external intervention. Families who have faced crises typically emphasize the importance of preparation and having a plan in place. Establishing a clear protocol for what to do in a crisis can alleviate panic and confusion. This may involve having contact information for mental health professionals readily available and understanding the signs that indicate a need for immediate assistance.

Lastly, the value of building a support network emerges as a vital lesson for all involved. Family members, friends, and caregivers benefit significantly from connecting with others who understand their experiences. Sharing personal stories and challenges can foster resilience and provide practical strategies for managing everyday life with bipolar disorder. Engaging with community resources, whether through support groups or educational workshops, allows families to learn from each other and gain insights that might not be found in isolation. These connections not only enhance understanding but also reinforce the notion that no one has to face the journey alone, promoting hope and healing.